Floods

BY TAMI DEEDRICK

Steadwell Books

Raintree Steck-Vaughn Publishers

A Harcourt Company

Austin · New York
www.steck-vaughn.com

Nature
on the
Rampage

Published by Raintree Steck-Vaughn Publishers,
an imprint of Steck-Vaughn Company.

Library of Congress Cataloging-in-Publication Data
Deedrick, Tami.
    Floods/by Tami Deedrick.
        p.c.m.--(Nature on the rampage)
    Summary: Explains what causes floods and what effects they
have on people's lives.
    ISBN 0-7398-1797-3
    1. Floods--Juvenile literature. [1. Floods.] I. Title. II. Series.
GB1399.D44 2000
363.34'93--dc21
                                                            99-058672

Printed in the United States of America
10 9 8 7 6 5 4 3 2 1 LB 02 01 00

Produced by Compass Books
Photo Acknowledgments
Archive Photos, 24, Reuters/Jeff Vinnick; Reuters/Str, 20;
Digital Stock, cover, 14, 15, 26
Photo Network, 18
Photophile/Jim Gray, 22
Unicorn, 11; Eric R. Berndt, 4; Aneal Vohra, 29
    (top)
Visuals Unlimited/W. Banaszewski, 8; Ken Lucas,
    10; A. Copley, 29 (bottom)

Content Consultant
Thomas H. Yorke
Chief, Office of Surface Water
U.S. Geological Survey

CONTENTS

▼ WATER POWER

Water sometimes flows onto normally dry land. This is called a flood. Floods kill people and destroy property. U.S. floods kill about 100 people each year. Floods cause more than $1 billion of property loss each year.

Water is a heavy, powerful force. Just 6 inches (15 cm) of fast-moving water can knock an adult off his or her feet. Water can pull down buildings and wash out bridges.

Water is one of nature's tools for shaping land. Moving water wears away rock and dirt. This process is called erosion. Moving water carved the Grand Canyon.

 Water that flows onto normally dry land is a flood.

EVAPORATION

The Water Cycle

Water covers 70 percent of Earth. Oceans, lakes, and rivers hold most of this water.

The water cycle lets nature use water again. Heat makes liquid water evaporate into water vapor. Clouds are made of water vapor. Water vapor cools and condenses. To condense means to change from a gas to a liquid form. Water falls back to Earth as rain or snow. The rain may gather in an ocean, lake, or river. Water evaporates again when it gets hot.

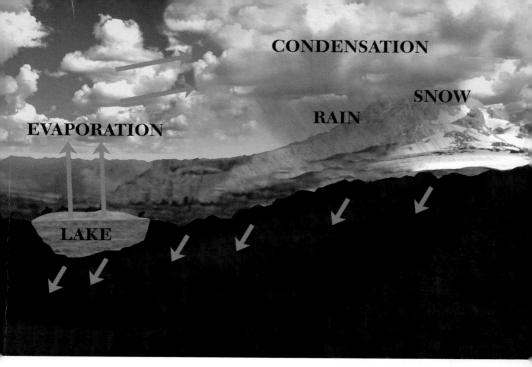

CONDENSATION

SNOW

RAIN

EVAPORATION

LAKE

▲ This diagram shows how the water cycle lets nature reuse water.

The water cycle keeps Earth's water sources fresh. Clouds bring water to dry places. This helps balance the amount of water on Earth. But sometimes the amount of water is not even. Not enough water can cause dry periods called droughts. Too much water may cause floods. The three kinds of floods are river floods, coastal floods, and flash floods.

 Floods can happen when dams break. Water has broken this dam.

River Floods

A river floods when water overflows its banks. Many things cause river floods. A river may not be able to hold extra water if too much rain falls.

Snow and ice can cause river floods. Snow and ice can melt and make too much water for a river to hold. Ice can also block rivers. Water flows around the block and floods land.

Rivers sometimes flood when dams or levees break. A dam is a wall built across a river to hold back water. A levee is a bank built along the side of a river. Water presses against dams and levees. Water can flow over a dam or levee or break through them. This releases large amounts of water that cause floods.

A flood plain is an area of low land near a river. People often build houses on flood plains. Floods often destroy houses on flood plains.

Dams

Dams may be made of earth, concrete, or rock. People make dams to hold back water. People release water from dams only when they want to. Some dams have special machines that make electricity when water is released.

Levees

Levees may be made of earth, concrete, or sandbags. People make tall levees on the sides of rivers to keep water in the rivers.

 Coastal floods can cause landslides.

Coastal Floods

Hurricanes and other large storms over the ocean can cause coastal flooding. The storms can bring much rain to ocean coasts. The storms may push waves of water over land. The flooding can also cause landslides.

Earthquakes and volcano eruptions also can cause coastal floods. The sudden shaking of the earth makes large ocean waves called tsunamis. These waves can wash over land and cause great damage.

▲ **Flash floods can wash away roads.**

Flash Floods

Much rain in a short time causes a flash flood. Flash floods often happen in mountains. The flood quickly races down slopes. It washes away mud, trees, animals, roads, and buildings. People who live in nearby valleys may have little warning. Flash floods often sweep away people's houses and cars.

Bad and Good

Floods can push heavy objects such as trees and cars into buildings. The objects can crush people. Rushing water can carry people or buildings away. It can throw them against rocks or bridges. People may drown.

People sometimes are in danger even after floods are over. Floodwater can make drinking water dirty. People can get sick from drinking it. Floods sometimes wash away crops. People who lose their crops may not have enough food to live.

Floods have some good uses. They clean out rivers and streams. Water pushes away trash and dead branches from river bottoms. Floods leave new nutrients in the soil. Nutrients are minerals that help plants grow.

Rushing water from the flooding Willamette River in Oregon is destroying this paper mill.

RIVER FLOODS

People sometimes build cities on flood plains near rivers. People use the river to move things in boats from city to city. People can drink or bathe in water from rivers. River floods leave rich soil on flood plains. Farmers can grow crops in the soil.

But living on flood plains can be dangerous. Rivers often flood. Floods have destroyed cities and crops. Fixing buildings damaged by floods can be costly.

A river flood damaged these houses that people built on the flood plain.

Flood Myths

Early people did not understand flooding. They told stories called myths to explain floods. They thought gods and goddesses caused floods.

• **In the Bible,** one famous flood story is about Noah. The story says God was angry. People were sinning. God told Noah to build a boat called an ark. Noah trusted God and built the ark.

God sent two of each kind of animal to Noah. Noah's family and the animals went into the ark. Then God sent rain for 40 days. Water covered the whole Earth.

Noah's ark landed on top of a mountain when the flood ended. God promised never to flood the whole Earth again.

• **In Italy,** the Romans told a flood story about Jupiter. He was angry because people were doing bad things.

Jupiter sent a flood. But he let two people live. He gave the two people stones. The people threw stones behind them. Each stone turned into a person. The new stone people helped rebuild cities.

• **In North America,** an American Indian group called the Pomo tell a flood story about Coyote. Coyote drank too much water and got sick. The medicine man came to help Coyote. He jumped on Coyote's stomach. The water flowed out of Coyote's mouth. It flooded the land.

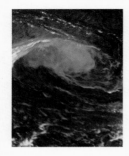

Flood Safety
Remember these safety tips during
a flood:
- Go to higher ground or climb to safety.
- Never take a vehicle on a flooded road.
- Do not try to walk or swim across a flooded area, even if you think the water is shallow.
- If the water reaches your ankles, turn around and go the other way. The water could knock you off your feet.

The Mississippi River Flood of 1993

The Mississippi River flood of 1993 was the worst flood in the United States. Heavy rains made the river rise. Levees broke. The Mississippi flooded 10 states.

Water flooded 16 million acres (about 6.5 million ha) of land. Water killed animals and washed away crops. The flood water ripped up graves in cemeteries. Coffins floated down the river.

The flood left 70,000 people homeless. About 50 people died.

The Nile River

The longest river in the world is the Nile River in Egypt. Nile floods were some of the first known floods. People in Egypt based their calendar on the flooding of the Nile. The floods left rich soil called silt on the ground. But the floods also destroyed many buildings.

In the 1950s, Egyptians decided to stop the floods. They built the Aswan High Dam to hold back the Nile's water.

The Aswan High Dam stopped the flooding. But it created new problems. The soil was not as good because floods did not leave silt on the ground. Crops did not grow as well. Some fish died because there was too much silt in the river's water. There were no longer floods to renew the Nile. The dam changed the way Egyptians use the Nile's water.

The Aswan High Dam holds back the Nile's water. People control how much water the dam lets flow.

▲ This Chinese family is homeless. Their house was flooded by the Chang Jiang River in July 1998.

Rivers in China

China has two long rivers that often flood. The Chang Jiang is the longest river in China. Chang Jiang also is called the Yangtze River. It rose 97 feet (30 m) above its usual level in 1931. The flood covered places with 20 feet (6 m) of water. It took two years for the water to dry.

About 4 million Chinese people died from the flood and famine. A famine is a lack of food. The flood washed away crops. The Chang Jiang still floods. In 1998, a flood there killed 4,150 people.

The second longest river in China is the Huang-He River. It also is called the Yellow River. Its water carries silt that makes the water look yellow. The river's nickname is China's Sorrow. The river's floods have killed more people than any other river floods on Earth.

The Huang-He flooded in 1887. Water swept away more than 1,500 towns. The flood left 6 to 8 feet (2 to 2.5 m) of sand on the flood plain. More than 1 million people died.

Chinese people are trying to control the river floods. The government has built dams to hold back the rivers' water. It has created large basins at the sides of the rivers. The basins hold extra water when the rivers get too high. Chinese people have built hundreds of miles of levees along the riverbanks. Each year, people work to make sure the levees stay in good condition. They add more dirt, rocks, and other materials to the levees. This makes the levees taller and stronger.

▼ Coastal and Flash Floods

People have tried to control floods by building dams and levees to hold back water. But coastal floods cannot be stopped with dams and levees.

Almost every year, large storms that start over oceans sweep over coastal areas. These storms bring unstoppable heavy rains and huge waves that cause floods. In 1999, Hurricane Floyd struck the east coast of the United States. It caused the worst flooding in North Carolina's history.

North America's most deadly coastal flood happened in 1900 in Galveston, Texas. On September 8, a hurricane pushed a 20-foot (6-m) high wave over the town. It created a deadly coastal flood. About 10,000 people died.

Large ocean waves often cause coastal floods. A coastal flood has covered this parking lot.

Bangladesh

Bangladesh is a country about 30 feet (9 m) above sea level. Sea level is the average level of the surface of the ocean. The country's low, flat land has often flooded. In 1970, more than 200,000 people in Bangladesh were killed by a coastal flood.

In 1988, Bangladesh had the worst monsoon in 70 years. A monsoon is a strong summer wind that brings very heavy rains. Three-quarters of the country flooded. Floods left 30 million people homeless. About 2,000 people died.

In 1991, Bangladesh flooded again. Waves more than 20 feet (6 m) high killed 150,000 people.

The Big Thompson River Flash Flood

The Big Thompson River is near Denver, Colorado. In July 1976, the river overflowed after five hours of heavy rain. Many people were camping in the Big Thompson Canyon.

A wall of water 20 feet (6 m) high rushed into the canyon. It swept away cars, buildings, and trees, and killed 140 people.

Heavy rain and a broken dam caused a flash flood that destroyed Johnstown, Pennsylvania.

Johnstown, Pennsylvania Flash Flood

On May 31, 1898, the South Park Dam in Pennsylvania broke after several strong storms. The rain and the broken dam caused a deadly flash flood.

A wall of water swept down from the dam to Johnstown, Pennsylvania. Moving water swept away railroad cars, houses, and whole forests. It washed away every building in two small towns. Fire started. It burned the floating trees and houses. About 2,200 people drowned or burned to death.

FLOODS AND SCIENCE

Scientists called hydrologists study water. They want to know when floods will happen. Scientists decide how much water rivers can hold. They check soil to see how much water it has.

In the United States, the National Weather Service gives flood warnings and watches. A flood watch means that flooding could happen soon. People should watch for bad weather. They should listen to the weather news during a flood watch.

A flood warning means a flood is happening or is about to happen. People should move to higher ground during a flood warning.

 This car was swept away in a river flood.

Flood Season

Floods are common during some times of the year. Many river floods happen during March or April. Winter snow melts during these months. Water from melted snow flows into rivers. August and September are common times for hurricanes and coastal floods. Hurricanes start over the ocean during these months.

People often have warning before coastal floods or river floods. Scientists can track big storms over the oceans. They warn people of approaching storms. People on coasts can get ready for flooding. Hydrologists measure the height of rivers to see if they are about to flood.

Scientists do not know when flash floods will strike. Flash floods happen with little warning. Scientists are teaching people to be more careful during heavy rain. New Doppler radar is helping scientists. This machine measures wind and rainfall amounts better than old radar systems.

Flooding will always be a part of nature. People can stay safe if they learn about flood safety. They should listen to flood watches and warnings.

Many river floods happen during March and April.

28

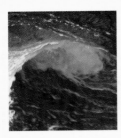

Saving Property

People can work together to reduce the harm from floods. People can pile sandbags along river banks to build levees. They can put sandbags around houses to stop water. People should tie down objects to keep them from floating away.

Glossary

ark (ARK)—a large boat

dam (DAM)—a strong wall built across a stream or river to hold back water

earthquake (URTH-kwayk)—a sudden shaking of the earth

flash flood (FLASH FLUHD)—flooding that happens quickly and without warning

flood plain (FLUHD PLANE)—low land near a river that often floods

hurricane (HUR-uh-kane)—a large, swirling storm with strong winds that starts over the ocean

levee (LEV-ee)—a bank built near a river to prevent flooding

monsoon (mon-SOON)—a strong summer wind that brings heavy rains

nutrient (NOO-tree-uhnt)—a mineral that helps plants grow

silt (SILT)—rich soil that is left on land when rivers flood

tsunami (soo-NAH-mee)—a large ocean wave that can cause great damage

National Water Information Clearinghouse
U.S. Geological Survey
423 National Center
Reston, VA 22092-0001

Water Education Foundation
717 K Street, Suite 517
Sacramento, CA 95814-3408

FEMA for Kids: Floods
http://www.fema.gov/kids/floods.htm

Floods in Focus
http://www.pbs.org/newshour/infocus/floods.html

The Living Almanac of Disasters
http://disasterium.com

Newton's Apple: Floods
http://ericir.syr.edu/Projects/Newton/12/Lessons/
    floods.html

INDEX